Other titles in the UWAP Poetry series (established 2016)

Our Lady of the Fence Post by J. H. Crone

Border Security by Bruce Dawe

Melbourne Journal by Alan Loney

Star Struck by David McCooey

Dark Convicts by Judy Johnson

Rallying by Quinn Eades

Flute of Milk by Susan Fealy

A Personal History of Vision by Luke Fischer

Snake Like Charms by Amanda Joy

Charlie Twirl by Alan Gould

Afloat in Light by David Adès

Communists Like Us by John Falzon

Hush by Dominique Hecq

Preparations for Departure by Nathanael O'Reilly

The Tiny Museums by Carolyn Abbs

Chromatic by Paul Munden

The Criminal Re-Register by Ross Gibson

Fingertip of the Tongue by Sarah Rice

Fume by Phillip Hall

The Flaw in the Pattern by Rachael Mead

Walking with Camels by Leni Shilton

Wildlife of Berlin by Philip Neilsen

I first saw these poems in manuscript when they were sent in to Radio National's Poetica program from the Cocos (Keeling) Islands and I knew they were important. It was not only their first-hand experience with refugees – though that was a big factor, as the plight of refugees is a defining feature of our times, and future generations will look back at our treatment of them and judge us as a people by it. It was also the geographical location of the poems and their sensitivity to an oceanic environment. Reneé Pettitt-Schipp has had an interest in the artistic and poetic movement known as Tidalectics, an ocean-based movement that seeks a more decentralised, environmental and fluid approach to world poetry and politics. The structure of the book follows a personal journey from Christmas Island, back to the Australian mainland to deal with the decline and death of her father, then to the Cocos (Keeling) Islands, and finally back to the suburbs of Perth. There is a restrained power in her lyrics and her political poems manage to be both trenchant and caring. In *The Sky Runs Right Through Us*, the sea unmakes our tight self-definitions and the margins become central. Reneé Pettitt-Schipp unsettles at the same time as she delights.

Mike Ladd

The Sky Runs
Right Through Us

Reneé Pettitt-Schipp

Reneé Pettitt-Schipp is an award-winning writer and educator living in Western Australia. From 2011 until 2014, Reneé lived on Christmas Island and the Cocos (Keeling) Islands in the Indian Ocean Territories, where she taught English and Art to asylum seeker and islander students. Reneé's recent work shares her experiences of living in our nation's most marginal territory, as well as her reflections on returning to the Australian mainland. Reneé's poetry has appeared in major Australian publications, multiple exhibitions, been recorded with singer-songwriters, as well as performed on national and local radio. Reneé has won or been shortlisted for many literary awards, including the ACU literature prize, the Dorothy Hewett manuscript award, the Grieve Poetry Prize, Ros Spencer poetry prize and the Trudy Graham Biennial literary award.

Reneé Pettitt-Schipp
The Sky Runs Right Through Us
Poems from the Edge of the Indian Ocean

First published in 2018 by
UWA Publishing
Crawley, Western Australia 6009
www.uwap.uwa.edu.au

UWAP is an imprint of UWA Publishing
a division of The University of Western Australia

This book is copyright. Apart from any fair dealing
for the purpose of private study, research, criticism
or review, as permitted under the *Copyright Act 1968*,
no part may be reproduced by any process without
written permission.
Enquiries should be made to the publisher.

Copyright © Reneé Pettitt-Schipp 2018
The moral right of the author has been asserted.

 A catalogue record for this
book is available from the
National Library of Australia

Designed by Becky Chilcott, Chil3
Typeset in Lyon Text by Lasertype
Printed by Lightning Source

 uwapublishing

To my father, Bill Pettitt,
for his difficult love,
and to my mother, Jan Little,
for coming on the journey
of forgiveness with me.

The heart that breaks open can contain the whole universe.
Joanna Macy

Contents

A Place Much Further 13

The Ocean of our Selves
This Same Humidity 16
Christmas Island 17
Midnight, Coming Home 18
Me. You. Us. 19
My Father Comes to the Island 21
The Politics of Entry 23
The Haunting 24
Parting Glass 25

In-Between Islands
The Colour of Friday 28
Stepping Through 29
Slow-Dancing 30
Measuring Loss 31
From the Train, by the River 33
In Praise of Worn Sneakers 34

Barely a Line Between Sea and Sky
Pinggir 36
Pinggiran 37
Echo 38
Termangu-Mangu 39
First Flight 40
Boys with Wings 41

West Island Walk, Sight of Syringes 42
Backpack 43
Soar 44
This Poem 45
Returning to Land 46
Weaving Ketupat on Pulu Cheplok 47
What Water Brings 48
Tiger on the Beach 49
The Will of Water 51

Sand Stays in Bathers on the Line
I. Return
Love Song 55
Bring your Armies 56
Return 57
Chlorine 58
Birdbath 59
Crow and Pylon 60
Song for Silence 61

II. Remember
Black Stone 64
Do They Still? 65
Dinner Table 66
Two Crows 67
Erase 68

I Eat the Day **69**
The Waiting Game **71**
Slate Cleaning **72**

III. We Are Cellular
New Eyes at Wet Night
Intersection **75**
Morning Prayer **76**
The Incredible Lightness of Being
(Magpie, 2011) **77**
Last Time I Saw You Your Hair Was
Long **78**
Somewhere Between a Thursday and
the Next **80**
Bright **81**
Cellular **82**
Autumn at the Cidery **83**
The Fact of You **85**
Watching a Beetle **87**
Gecko **89**

IV. Shift
Shift **91**
Last Tree East on Hartley Street **92**
Standing Under Stars **95**
Catching the Sun **96**
Dozing Cat **97**
Tongue to the Wind **98**

Fig Tree in Passing **99**
Derbarl Yerrigan Addresses Mooro
Katta **100**
Kings Park **101**
Park in Spring **102**
Redtails **103**

V. Perspective
Grass Tree in Sunlight after
Rain **105**
So That I May Ask the Morning **106**
The Sky Runs Right Through Us **107**
Love Letter **108**
Cabbage Moth **109**
What the Rain Said **110**
Fitzroy Crossing **111**
He Sat with a Stone and Called it
Love **112**
Perspective Passes over Us **113**
Smog, Delhi (2016) **114**
In Delhi They Let Sleeping Dogs
Lie **115**
Tuesday Waits in Lodtunduh **116**
Song to Self **118**

Notes **120**
Acknowledgements **121**

my father planted this ocean in me
a childhood semi-submarine
summer's halo, waiting all winter
to return to the water with him

A Place Much Further

this land's edge
has always been an invitation
a white-toothed smile
to walk on

take a step
the earth's layer will not mind it
will sweep our footprints over and again
like a wound healed instant

your warmth   wide sky
wondering how to say I'd take
                       your hand

but the land claimed you first
threw up gardens in us
until we sprouted colour   lived like light
                     her shade grew

a thousand times   this land's edge
           you and I

the shore doesn't mind   sweeps
our prints over
like a wound undone

we turn toward the air of its invitation
a place much further than our eyes can see
                 take this hand   step up
                             step off

The Ocean of our Selves

(Christmas Island)

This Same Humidity

after the borrowing
the fracturing, rain
returns the ocean
to itself
this drawing in
surrenders distinction
between sea and sky, blurs
their bold titles
with one rich smear

inside
your skin, a scent
like belonging
the rhythm of you breathes
to me all night
in this same humidity
the oceans of our selves condense
and with each body's slow
sweat we bleed
our beginnings.

Christmas Island

below us
rock plummets to depths
we cannot hold true
while all else thrusts skyward
with the violence
of uprising

we sit on this delicate
formation of faults
that quakes and quivers
with change and witness
life wanting life –
with each red claw

the wind breathes
back to the sea
with each turtle's lumber
up the slow sand
speaks an ancient will
to continue

like each new boat
buoyed and heavy with hope
just one dance;
the grace of the willing.

Midnight, Coming Home

palm trees paint darkness
onto darkness
thong-step slap
against silence

so alone
first time
I have known
high stars, black street
no fear

Me. You. Us.

There are twenty-seven young Afghan men
that come to our makeshift school
in the afternoon.
At first I battle to tell them apart;
the Mohammeds, Alis and Ali Rezas.

Today is their third day
the guard brings me three
sixteen- and seventeen-year-old boys.
We sit in the demountable
by the whir of an ancient air conditioner.
On the window painted wire
forms thin bars.

We look at
letter sounds and names
pronouns, proper nouns, conjunctives.
They are struggling
to form the *n* sound, so I show them
a little self-consciously
how my tongue is positioned
behind by teeth.
The students try,
furrow their brows and try again
until the strange task
has us eye to eye, laughing
in one language.

Suddenly they seem so close
the blood and breath of them.
I look toward Ali and see the shape
of his eyebrows
notice the way they thicken then disperse
the gradations of brown in his iris
when lit by the light from the window.

I witness the wounds crudely stitched
that run up Mohammed's arm
until they disappear beneath
his shirt sleeve.
I inhale the warmth of Mussa
his scent of cigarettes, spice and sweat.

The music teacher arrives
with drums, CDs and a whiteboard marker.
Together the students sing,
'I am, you are, we are Australian'.
I turn and quickly leave the room.

My Father Comes to the Island

my father comes to the island
we turn it between us
the new shape
of him

in gentle morning light
I see him dressing, through his
half-opened door
reading in stark ribs
what neither one of us
can say

my father, once amphibian
his swimmer's feet now numb
crash blindly into coral, silent
the limp and bleed
of each day

my father comes to the island
pulls cap over new sight of scalp
though we both know
what's written
under there

standing by the wire
he and I watch his plane come in
I hold him closer than ever

he walks away from me
and still I don't say
I don't say
a thing.

The Politics of Entry

Coming in the back door
like you could wait politely at the front one.
Coming in the back door
like survival was a party, you're just not invited.
Yet in all this facelessness
there is the coming from;
coming from a landscape in shadow
where rape is tactical, procedural, political
hold the daughter still
plant your flag in that dark place,
force the life out of her eyes until she
is pregnant with the violence of it.
Let despair grow round
and firm and hungry.
We say; the welcome mat,
red carpet, flood gates open
when all you see is light
from darkness
a door ajar

The Haunting

on our island, the young girl's ghost
curls beneath the nightscape

by the toilets, the young girl's ghost
has some in tears

on our island, what's by the toilets
stops men leaving their rooms
on our island, by the toilets
a tiny ghost

on our island, behind the wire
between the guards the Afghans see
a girl's ghost by the toilets
her unwet tears

men will not leave
their cramped and rotting dorms
cannot stand to hear the sound
of her suffering.

Parting Glass

after Gabriela Mistral

for M., asylum seeker and friend, who attempted to take his own life at North West Point Detention Centre Christmas Island, 2011.

the act is simple enough
remove lid from bottle
pour into plastic cup
pour like rain at midnight
a river's sheen by firelight
your childhood framed in puddles
like a dream

the liquid claims light like
a jungle newly varnished
bright fishing boats in moonlight, until
ocean deep with dawn
like a prayer

lift the vessel high
to all you've ever known
close those eyes
to lovers and glances
music and dancers
beautiful hunger
shiver of sky

and in that moment
when rim meets
your mouth
relinquish
outstretched arms, eyes
of nieces
pull of letters

your own face

then swallow
there will be searing
like villages blazing
plumes from boats
wire and want
ablaze

gulp
at new dark freedom
promise of oblivion, after pain
when this world sways
leave the afterglow

without your name.

In-Between Islands

The Colour of Friday
(living with my brother)

I pulled the blind chord
and the whole thing came down
a shocking cacophony of wood.
You walk into the room one sock
already pulled over your jeans leg
lean your bike on the wall so we
can raise it up to the sill, then
the daylight dims
and you are gone.

On the veranda in the morning sun
golfers stand on infant hills
with wide strides alongside magpies.
In the sure light
my coffee stews, steam curls
around new rays
around the ring on my finger, strident
nagging at my retinas
until I relent
and agree; the world
somehow
still golden.

Stepping Through

I'm not one for words
my father tells me
and the lines of the port slip by;
bold containers, blue road of river
crane extending arm
                to the sky

he's not one for words, but women
they can go on and on
that's not his way, he says
and I slow
stop at the lights, thinking
we don't have much time

I say, I know you love me
turn to him in my seat
he laughs, eyes widen
holds my gaze
something opens, my father
                      steps through

Slow-Dancing

we drive my father to the water
he takes his time
even asks for help, though
be subtle, he says

at ocean's edge
with familiar gusto
my father dives into memory
sister and I
turn our gaze
        away

while we wait
Dad backstrokes into aqua
I try not to fold, hold
the world steady
on sand

coming back
we walk together
      shuffling steps
his arms around
our necks
over rise and fall
pothole and root
      slow-dancing
          waltzing our way
        to the end.

Measuring Loss

there are books about perfect endings
beings who reach an ease with eternity
who slip into sleep so profound
but today by your bed in the suburbs
ours is an ordinary grief

it's the way I contain
a measure of your loss
each time it's my hand
that brings the cup's rim
to your lips

it's the brute strength it takes
to haul your thin frame
up the pillows
how I cannot meet your eyes
when the muscle
is mine

it's how
with sudden certainty
we know your legs
will unlearn their walking
how you cannot eat
strain to speak
how you cannot

I watch you wade
through your sea's dull pain
the way it sharpens with you in its wake
making you wake, and again wake
until I am measuring morphine
knowing exactly
what that means

yesterday at sunrise
we made our slow way up the hill
where for a moment
a pair of kites wore your wings
over needles and cones
we watched their tender dance
you stole their bodies
borrowed flight

but now, back here
where sunflowers nod
and magpies pull
worms unwatched
I wonder whether
to touch you, again
lift that mug to your mouth
as high in pines
a redtail screams

From the Train, by the River

a landscape of shadow
just-light of dusk, silhouette
of nine swans moving as one
over grey-shine of water

small wings work hard
against near night, necks still
drawn thin, nine lines
of longing

In Praise of Worn Sneakers

yesterday
I did not know
how to begin

but this morning
sitting on a thin edge
of bed, I followed a line of lace
to my shoes
and knew

see how they own their purpose
these things of sole and synthesis
how they slide over feet
memory corporeal, imprinted
with history shared

the invitation is too tangible
to refuse, so the shoes
return me to places from before
hold me, firm
my one foot
in front
of the other.

Barely a Line Between Sea and Sky

(Cocos (Keeling) Islands)

Pinggir

With many thanks to Pak Yati, Mak Sofia and Pak Greta
for the translations into Cocos Malay.

apa arti nya hidup sekejap saja
di atas lautan...

what does it mean to live   subsist   just a moment
above the ocean   where the slow coral
grows its mighty mountain   and life explodes
as atoll meets air

all night I hear the sea's
secret undoing   all day witness
uncountable beings
rebuild

some early evenings when the sun is stirred
into the trees   and the water returns
to reclaim its margins   *kami sepi*
we are still

only then will crabs appear   bodies below
in air their eyes   between worlds
like sharks pushing fins
into sky

here the sea's skin looks
like something you can trust
the statement of its reflected surface
is sure   promises we belong
above.

Pinggiran

seperti hujan terbalek
like rain inversed
tiny fish
push into air
bodies showering toward
high cloud

tempat ini adalah milik
sendirian
this place belongs
to itself
you arrive on its terms
remain terrestrial   peripheral

kehidupan belum tentu
life is tenuous
here on the merest
suggestion of soil
that contracts

expands
with the lagoon's
slow exhalation

a rhythm we all
wait for
live by
har-hari ter gantung
days poised
on the rush of its breath.

Echo

...the birds have also all but gone from South Keeling...it is all too easy to believe [they] were never present in any great number...
Armstrong, 1991

I miss skies
full of birds

it makes the clouds
seem like
their own desert places

these wild spaces echo
with loneliness

Termangu-Mangu*
after Neil Young

the earth curves here
relentless horizon
edges that never
               end

absence of anchors   only
shift and surge
play of light
where I can't
lose your eyes

out on the water   so quickly
we lose sight of land
day dissolves
cells thin and disperse
      world unwitnessed by you
        I am unmade   undone
                    falling
                  off the face
                  of the earth.

* *sad, and unsure what to do*

First Flight

An asylum-seeker vessel carrying 63 passengers has arrived off the Cocos Islands...Arrangements are being made to transfer the... refugees to Christmas Island
The Australian, May 16 2012

my home faces the runway
a thin blue line
only herons can cross

today you are our island's
new cargo   dark figures
under thick sun

I am all eyes
at the end of my driveway
behind me kettles and printers, dryers and freezers
form a crowd of everyday anchors
while you are dwarfed on the tarmac
alone   beneath haze of sky

engines roar and crescendo
a flash of bright white wing
then you are climbing, climbing thin air

and I watch in wonder
and as I watch   how must you feel
how do you feel
right   now?

Boys with Wings

a terrible insect
the military plane
drags us from sleep

all over our island its deafening whine
seeks out silence   ends conversations mid-
word   dull machinery raging against the wind

that afternoon   by the ocean
the two pilots arrive bringing their drifting eyes;
a man's gaze   yet with bone white skin
and adolescent arms   the pair seem
hatched   newborn

detached by slice of sea
one bright head tells me his facts about flying
about last night   the Sri Lankan boat   alone
in a place in the ocean   where ocean
is all that there is

says   *it should be here by tomorrow afternoon*   adds
that is   if it comes at all   and I wonder if he knows
what he means.

West Island Walk, Sight of Syringes

almost overnight
        currents change
    and with them arrives
a new wave
of dark gifts that sink
their sharp facts
into sand

toes bare   I consider
their measured and hollow
selves   the finer
points of addiction
an unknown
elsewhere   its rising
            tide

Backpack

new flotsam is arriving outside my home
nylon beings with textured flaps
that extend over crests of waves
contract again   until
beached   they adopt attitudes
of abandon

sometimes I watch these bags for days
              caught between the breakers
          and the backflow
                    oscillating between

when they finally achieve their mute arrival
I rummage through their pockets like a thief
tugging at their zips   a little ashamed
looking for a clue   for a trace

but hostile seas ensure
each story stolen
life erased.

Soar

But there is one charming bird: a small, snow-white tern, which smoothly hovers at a distance of a few feet above one's head, its large black eye scanning, with quiet curiosity, your expression.
Charles Darwin, during his visit to the Cocos (Keeling) Islands, 1836

we raised the tern the pilot found
with minute wings and shock
of down, jumble of filigree bones, alone
his utter and necessary trust

roly-poly his balled body
teetered at the end of our couch
one eye watching you, pen in mouth
homework spreading up and out

we witnessed suspensions, hoverings
      flurry of pale wings
our laughing mouths, his untrained grace
        mapping the paths
between us all

the day you left
he could not circle
your homecoming head
in the driveway

the day you left
amongst frangipani blooms
he sat brilliant, bridal
waiting

This Poem

These poems are not patient with me, they will not wait for a convenient time, they wrestle in my blood like tempestuous twins and demand to be fed, to be fed. These poems are not ones for waiting they pierce my dreams and beg to be born, call the ocean in from the window. These poems are not dormant, sleeping, silently gestating, they are emboldened, fat, fertile from living on a lip of land made and unmade each day by sweeping gestures of ocean, by this shout of sky and parade of life that crawls and schools, feeds and rules this creeping crater.

  This poem is slowing now, having eaten sleep I could have saved, having scrawled its life across my page,
      having felt its lung, having birthed, become,
         having won.

Returning to Land

it is hard to feel real in this postcard place
barely a line between sea and sky

it feels almost a burden, this scene
perfect and mine alone, an extravagant gift
from an unnamed sender

as I walk into water schools part before me
beneath the surface constellations of neons
blaze over bright moons of coral

warm as a womb, suspended in silence
I drift, know on this atoll I will always
                              be arriving

returning to land the wind shifts, stirring
high fronds, bringing shadow. Behind me
a shark traces my scent to shore

on the horizon
boats are burning.

Weaving Ketupat on Pulu Cheplok

the neneks are starting to weave
laughing under thin palms
quick fingers, memory of muscle
mast tap-tapping in breeze

laughing in shade of thin palms
Nek splits fronds with sure fingers
mast tap-tapping in breeze
soft parcels piling by feet

sure hands, movement of muscle
boat rocking slow in shallows
Nek invites me to weave
from banana-lounge under lean tree

boat sways, slaps sides on cool water
the neneks are patient with me
pale palm over and under
these fingers cannot remember
Trade Winds coming over sea.

What Water Brings

we are learning archaeologies of loss
rummaging along edge of island
turning each gift left by the tide

meanwhile, unseen at the edge of the atoll, fifty-eight
Tamils are escorted in; navy ship grey, fishing boat festive
jubilant in sunlight

within the lagoon's still waters officers
insist on life jackets, clothing refugees
in orange irony

from SIEV to zodiac, zodiac to Customs, Customs to shore
shore to bus, they are watched, guided, guarded
a headline brews

but here we are oblivious, searching amongst the seaweed
finding thongs, whole bulbs and bottles, a toy soldier
minus his head

later, we drive through palms beneath tall towers of cloud,
past the Quarantine Station where the bus has just arrived
and the dust will not settle.

Tiger on the Beach

we round the point, run into
the plate-glass shock
of your presence
who designed
the monstrous fact of you?

who engineered the slipstream sinews
the meeting of muscles that steels
your formidable form?
Sea tiger, *kua,* shark chief, *na 'aumakua*
why are you lying so still
on the shore?

we find you fin first
discover you from the architecture
the angle of your tilted tail
even your stench is impressive
finger over nostril, hand over mouth
I pace your presence from end to end

how can it be
that your plain potency
cannot flick the fly, the crab?

your skin has begun to wrinkle, echoes
the pattern on the ocean floor
becomes fingertips of children at bath time
but on your lonely shore, sea abandoned
the tide is out

I slide one forefinger over your flesh
my muscles tensed and irrational
the terrain of your skin
a sea of serrations
resisting my touch

your prised jaws
closed like a finished sentence
your trophy teeth hidden
lending you an alien softness
wide-eyed, full-faced
open

and your one quiet eye
amber and turned to the sun
what did it last see?
what kind of parting gift
did the light leave?

then there it is
above the eye, the mark
that makes me see
skin cold
I read where the blade
drove in and in
          and in

The Will of Water

Out beyond ideas of wrongdoing and rightdoing,
there is a field. I'll meet you there.
When the soul lies down in that grass,
the world is too full to talk about.
Rumi

out beyond the reef
beyond the horizon, beyond
the breakers
there is a space
that will break
that will break, that will
unmake you

out beyond the breakers
beyond borders, tankers, Customs
freighters
out beyond eyes
beyond sight and the light
of conscience

hear the timbre of strain
sing a low, sad song
this vessel was never meant
to contain such weight

out in the middle of
we will decide who comes
and in the thick of *the circumstances*
every fear of each imagined ending
will engulf you
for we are a land that will not
(a line that will not)
give

out where mothers
are grasping for children's limbs
we are losing patience with pity, turn away
we will not witness, it will not stick
for we did not see
heard no screams
let me wash my hands
I know nothing
of the will of water

out beyond the ocean
and all its undoing
you had a dream. I will meet you there
for when each life is at last allowed its living
the world will be too full
to write about.

Sand Stays in Bathers on the Line

(From the Mainland)

I. Return

Love Song

I cannot say what it is

but I have been circling it lately like a bird honing in on home, my wings sing with its sight, with the steady song that pulses through sky

round and round I circle on its updraught, learning its rhythms, its sounds lifting wings the wind's clean on my face so I stay with the source of this song

love and I, we are getting to know each other properly. Moving ever so slightly through her song-scape, I start to think of twigs and branches, but I do not think that love is a place where you can rest

so I work to be with love, I listen and I listen, soaring through her song, trying to be ready, to pay attention. She is patient with me, we move together and I know one day

she will have me whole.

Bring your Armies

paper-thin   summer leaves curl   forming eager cups
bleached buffalo   forms a lawn of swords

where I have come from   nimbus roll in   armies of shadow
massing on horizon   above the atoll's whisper of sand

but here there are roots   and the earth is ancient and deep
sturdy   terrestrial and sure

as I stand hose in hand   I feel the Marris searching
blindly reaching down
                    down

calling to that other world of water
bring your dark armies   their sharp arrows of rain.

Return

Shelley Beach

this is what you will
come back to

the only way in
is down
the only way in
is water

this is what you've
always known   subsurface
liquid pixels of summer-blue
holding you

here it's what still holds you
all lines in the landscape
lead to this

it is to live for
your place amongst
the smallness of things
unquestionable

while a landscape never longs
or waits for anyone

the water
takes you back   despite
everything.

Chlorine

the smell of my love for you
matching Adidas tracksuits and thongs

my eyes counter-height
and you with your lean blue bag –
its goggles, towel and soap
broad body entering water
a bear honing in on home

and I'd kick like mad to keep up with you
to keep pace with your adult life
better than a boy I would be
the water alive with light

this is the sight of my love for you
crochet of sun across tiles blue
warping in waves the straight black line
where I still follow you

Birdbath

unblinking eye
in its gaze
beaks dive and drink
each brief life

between the immense
and this moment
such a brief
and tender whispering

I see
I am already water
become
each beak.

Crow and Pylon

The crow is the black the clouds can't match, feathers still gloss-bright in thwarted light. It splays its wings – gloved hands, feathered fingers, reaches, grips pylon high on hill. There is something in the pylon now gripped by the crow that seems like arrival. It stops me on the front steps as clouds turn gouache, and the wires, their sky lines, run eyes on tracks back to this. The crow calls, is joined by another, then another, and I see it is always here the birds return, swirling around its spire, twenty or thirty dark lives, like they know too what I can't say

Song for Silence

*The silence
that lies like a baby bird between your hands
your only friend.*
Rolf Jacobsen

all year I have waited for silence
like a farmer waits for rain
angling my ear like he would
his eye

all year I have waited for darkness
to reach me once again
wrap its deep arms around me
call it rest

and as night pulls down its blind
of stars   the bold orb cuts clear
above me   round mouth a cold gasp
held

these days I do not wait
for invitations   but the want
in body wills me   to a place the precise
shape of sleep

standing now on the moon's
surprised surface   amidst an enormous
nothing   space beyond horizon
winking, humorous stars

here I push my feet
into a cold I've never known
on a surface spurned
by sun

monochrome   I raise my arms
into impossible absence
and my ears sing
the hush

I am a new shoot
in this world of ancients
I inhabit the status
of ants

while all around   this orchestra
of everything   haze and halo
where even light
has aged

and where for a moment
the indifference of rock
becomes a brilliant
home   until

I lose all anonymity
back behind walls
steeped in sun   contained
by familiar gravity.

II. Remember

Black Stone

this stone that you have given me
is for the carrying

it will not leave me though I place it
under bushes, beside bus stops, throw it out to sea

I have worried it, fingered its surface so long
I've eroded angles, ended edges, weathered words

the day you should have turned seventy
I brought it out into sunlight in your park

so settled, it seemed, fragment fitting my palm
its black weight nestling sadness into skin

black as it was, the light still leaned to rub against it
the world to love it, until its tiny dark heart

sang.

Do They Still?

do they still light the fire in the room of my childhood?
do the sheoaks thread jewels on slender leaves
is fear still framed behind bannisters?

do ghosts bake bread in the kitchen
do children still laugh up limbs
and cry in bed?

does the paving crack like a sleepy
earthquake above the will of roots
can you hear a golden whistler?

or have our million steps been stripped
with the carpet and all our sadness
been paint-silenced white?

have all the axolotls left
for Mexico and the darkness
shattered with new life?

Dinner Table

mastication
was not something talked
about in my family
we were to do it
quietly
with our mouth shut
or you can do it
in the chook shed
our Dad said
but I'd carried
the question for days, so
serve it up, unceremoniously
with dinner:
what's a wanker?
sudden silence
wonder at my new word
its world of mystery
my brother's face
deepest of reds.

Two Crows

on a summer lawn
after rain

delinquent company
in blue-black jackets
muscular and adolescent

blatant   sharp-
eyed   vital and bold

the violence
in their glances.

Erase

1993

the body is one great experiment
and when I put mine before you

I died a small death   in that white-washed cabin
confusing directness with honesty

in that moment   when your hardness demanded an answer
I felt my face erase

I died a small death   while the boat rocked and moaned
I died a small death
             underneath you.

I Eat the Day

like clockwork
I do it
I simply push
the morning's
hard white form
from its place
then bring that small
promise to my lips
every week
I bring Monday
to my mouth
smooth, spherical
ready-as-a-mint
and I
am grateful
it makes every
morning a decision
to go without, though it
seems like a mean-ness
a small withholding
a slap to my body's
fine technology
this morning
is Wednesday, perfect
perforated, framed by foil
but despite this
enamelled independence
I can't help wonder
at these small endings;

each refusal
a curt, rushed parting
before we even
began.

The Waiting Game

round the corners of love's making
you are forming a story of your own

rising on the sure tides of a sealed world
you are remember-less, timeless
in your expression of something
infinite

you are the hope of your species
growing, fruit of prayers
unspoken

you are the anchor
in a chanced, fleeting meeting –
a plus, a bigger *us*

you are your own sweet secret
owning my body like
a border

you are a stranger already welcomed,
you are what you will be
and we are
waiting.

Slate Cleaning

the impossible
sum: 1+1= 3
then multiply
for in my daughter's
new eyes I see
my mother, and her
mother's mother
smile
my true disciple
follows me around the garden
with her cross-legged crawl
monkey on my back
while I plant lobelias
bittersweet
for I am also *daughter*
this one failing
at forgiveness, dark
and wearing a ripening
rage.

My daughter's skin
is a clean slate to the sun
her blue-sponge eyes
soak up the world
as if the moon and sun
applaud her sleep and rising
she throws half words at birds
and expects them to join her
on the grass

swathed in white towelling, seems
small prophet of the pure
her face reflects
the light.

III. We Are Cellular

New Eyes at Wet Night Intersection

it is you that makes me stop and think
the full round red drama of you
stronger than a bushfire moon
a setting sun, Monet's apple
and in knowing that it is fleeting
your little hexagons of light before

green and I'm gone, less likely to consider
the similes and metaphors of the 'go' globe
until orange as an orange I am
back to where I started thinking
bushfire moon, setting sun, Monet's apple

the thin lines of tar that bandaid
the street run like red rivers
under your red light
and all ordinary struck by this moment's
new hue

but it was when the moon
sat behind your red, orange, green
I caught my breath and
it seemed
there was nothing more perfect
nothing more lovely
nothing more pure and whole and right
than this white, red, orange, green
moon and traffic light.

Morning Prayer

the sun sends prayers down my street
one ray at a time   washes the world with wonder   says again
begin

the spider catches its meaning
raindrops shimmering wildly   beaded in her net
where she waits

from web   drops sink to soil
still holding firm that promise   each giving up their gold
to the ground

the soil finds this hope
draws in its rich suggestion   and takes its deeper question
to the seed

the seed sings with surprise
its answer all green and wanting   asks the sun for more and then
still more

so the sun rises higher
rises higher still   until the world is bold with blue
and all I have to do

is say
Amen.

The Incredible Lightness of Being
(Magpie, 2011)

from red-tile roof the young bird calls
a strong, descending warble
he is lighter than me, bolder
with his stark coat and definite beak

he grips my neighbour's aerial never once
lamenting it is not a tree.

Last Time I Saw You Your Hair Was Long

I don't know how it should work,
driving down the South West highway, thinking your
bundle of flesh and bones is in cold storage somewhere
while we race back through the heat to help make
arrangements

I think of the thin pile of you
stacked against beige pillows and us trying
to rearrange you
prop you on your spine in front of your
white cut sandwiches, crusts off
blinking as you ate them slowly like a tired child

your hair, always perfectly set
(audience or no) kept bothering you
tenderly I stroked it into a bun
and I think you were glad though
you thought I was my mother, 'Jan' you said

Christmas and we left you
alone in that cubicle
worrying about the spider
behind the light
Christmas and we left you
inserted between pastel screens
we three believing we had
little choice

at the door we forgot the code to
get out and laughed saying
'imagine we could not leave.'

Somewhere Between a Thursday and the Next

I didn't know he had family
they all arrive today, park on the verge
in new cars – would've shined
but for the sky

I didn't know he had family
only heard him coughing
tried to wave when I put the bins out
neighbourly, but for the eucalypts between

They go in, the late one
drives the wrong way down
this one way street, checks his phone
they open boots, talk facing
into that dark space
go back inside

In the morning
the cleaning lady arrives
and I realise
in the early light she shakes
all memory in the sun

By Thursday
a man with his sign
that says
all is up for sale.

Bright

all day the flowers have been
opening bright mouths to bees
bees read their words like braille
make fingers of fine feet
carry all those yellow stories home

in branches honeyeaters
walk slim stalk ladders   new leaves
push like thank yous into light
we forget roots deep
and silent

at this ceasing of colour
day's end is a small grief
but the wagtail softens
offers an evening song

and my dream ears will catch
clear notes of mopokes
while to the night
the moon shape whispers o
and then o.

Cellular

Bicton Baths

Dad, I walked with you down the river today, or some sense of you steeping water, written into flesh. Where the jetty's boards are drying in the sun, in its fibres, all those stories held of you; trapped beneath the surface, tide too high, rush of burning in lungs as timber stops your head from rising. The shark that passed you by. Slow syrup from the sugar factory, swimming in its warm and steady current. A small school of fish group in the yellow shallows, their tiny lives. I want to show you, instead you stay with me, in my bones, in the strong shoulders you left behind.

    At edge of jetty I stop, sit in light and as it happens sometimes, a pod of dolphins make unhurried arcs above the surface. It is then I think with you, down curved lines of their spines, with shine of fin, I own your eyes. And it's not the thought of you floating above me, not your heart beating in each bird's chest, but in my step, the memory of your muscle, in my breath, all your breaths before. This is how you walk with me; heel, ankle, shin, thigh, only ever partly mine. You with and so far from me, your life quicksilver out into the world, the murmurations left behind.

Autumn at the Cidery

Bridgetown

autumn
we don't own it
the way the sun is sleeping
in the leaves
sky boasting again about colour
and our love like a clear note
just sung

we sit with all this
and our tenderness curls
like a satisfied cat   gaze turned
out toward the river-gums
where dragonflies move like laughter
and butterflies descend
in slow sentences

and I am just about to think
perhaps there is perfection
only not sustained   more like flashes
of pure white light

when seeds   soft stars
begin falling
constellations earth bound
and shining

stunned in our seats   lulled by pale ale
pacified by their gentle persuasion
we let it happen
a landscape taken by siege
the bulrushes
           floating.

The Fact of You

this body does not
make much sense
without the fact of you; for what
all this curving and softness
for what this haze of hair?
you stand on the opposite
side of earth
the air in our lungs must
feel different
the sun takes its turns
with us

it is calm here
it is a broad, clean space
where you are
not

the days pass with order

I do not feel halved, but hungry
for the soft-eyed warm light
the red heart of you;
for the song
the strum of you
your clear, rich notes
when my head touches the pillow
I sleep
with the birds, I wake

I eat, I dress, drink coffee
in the morning sun

but as I
turn in the shower
I wish the offering
of your open hand
would come and define
a body that remembers

and waits.

Watching a Beetle
Beeliar Wetlands

I watch the beetle make her slow way along the path
her journey knows every rise in concrete
every sweep of mortar

there is something so simple
about how she does what she does, moving each of her six legs
her fine antennae, knowing only this, then this, then that

I wish I had fine antennae to help me feel my way forward
six legs to know the earth. I wish I knew how to slow my days
my minutes, into one foot in front
of the other

yesterday the first of the machinery
moved into the wetland
thirty people ran to witness
twenty police to meet them
I imagined the black cockatoo stirring in his tree
the oblong tortoise speeding over base of lake

(all the things I want to say are robbed by cliché
all the things I want to know take time)

that night, someone set fire to the lake's bushland
its flames spread through tall stalks
drying in the suggestion of summer
the blaze was soon quenched, but something
dark has burnt into me
                      yet

all the while
the moon is resting on someone's skin, a father leans,
kisses his daughter's head, honeyeaters
are suspended in light above a sprinkler
I want to wander with the beetle, to know just this
and what to do next, how to walk toward what it is
                              that feeds me.

Gecko

Married to the rock, you are the sun-soaker, quivering
with life. Married to earth you move like air, you have no
business with betweens. Quicksilver, you map mountains
of trees, of walls and windows. But here in the sun you
have stopped, your silent eye takes me in whole.
I wonder how I seem; not log, not bird, not branch.
You think with wood and become it, betrayed by your tiny heart
bursting its beats, bold beneath your skin.

IV. Shift

Shift

Donnelly River

it leans on us, this heavy sky
this season of wait
where Karri foliar shadows
shift and darken

the sawmill has been abandoned
no tree, no house will go near it
leaving an exposed wound of pit-red gravel
and all that timber falling, falling in on itself
fenced like regretting
the silence cordoned

and all the while its stories slip
frame by wooden frame
returning to the earth a fraction
of what it owes.

Last Tree East on Hartley Street

7.27
winter-pale
light at dawn
two trucks, one trailer
and a red four-wheel drive
these are the
only signs

7.32
day's slow dawn
shatters
as machinery
mulches the silence
outside our lounge
pale limbs are shaking
as tree is tied
ladder laid along
its length

it used to be
hard to soak
this sun in the morning
trees to the east so fat with foliage
the day had to introduce itself
slowly
in shards and winks
each leaf lifting, longing
for first light

then the Marri went
like it had walked away
next neighbours had to subdivide
leaving a massive slice of sky
where the whitetails had
once learned their lines
or else
were silent

but its 7.47
at last-tree-left
not native, not ancient
just a delicate filigree of leaves
to soften the fact of evening and
the sight of all that light
leaving

7.48
there is laughing now
camaraderie amongst carnage
as those long limbs
stop their shaking
stop their quivering
reach up, then out
and are gone

7.52
trucks and trunks
have disappeared
looking out of our cold windows
the sun is rising higher
shines in our eyes
like it meant it, as if
for a moment
we are blind.

Standing Under Stars

1.
after that time   or because of it   he buys the girls
dirt bikes for Christmas   in the afternoon light
their red-blonde hair flares back   soft tendrils reaching out

2.
raising children is easy he assures me   doesn't know
what these single mums are on about   from his
wound-down window offers me a wolf-whistle   thinks it's a gift

3.
there should be trumpets   marching bands   the morning she returns
instead the pair of them ride up and down   calling *Mum! Mum!*
then on the dawn of a sleepless night   she is gone

4.
three pm Sunday   different daytime shouting
his drinking legs won't walk   his cries crack
with the sound   of a man afraid of dying

5.
before Christmas   again sleepless nights   this time
a deeper shade of shadow   hands shaking I am listening
standing under powerlines   breathing low   a sky of silent stars

6.
at ten pm   he takes out the bin   our meeting eyes blaze
he raises his chin   thrusts out his chest   and I face him
show I can see   in all that darkness.

Catching the Sun

the corellas are returning
                early this evening   and curious

they fly
        white and brilliant
                right above my crouched form
                        in the garden

turning their heads as they pass
                they crane to make sense
                      of my strange evening task
                              below

tonight
      the sky is still astounding
              still brilliant with blue
                    as they make their raucous way
                              home

they are a carnival
          a canopy of white
                    one hundred new canvases
                              stretching
                                    for the sun.

Dozing Cat

inside your soft shell, that
strong heart

you are surrendered to sun
in the late afternoon's corner while

your body is busy
being alive, your invisible

pulse keeps time with the song
of your life, paced by the day's hue

you contract, then again
such soft expansion

I know you can't smile, but surely
one eye closing

is a wink.

Tongue to the Wind

Yesterday afternoon driving down Stock Road, I was delighted by a dog in a ute, face to the wind. I resist the urge to say he smiled, though his enormous tongue hung sideways out the long line of his mouth, and in his black-furred body, his pleasure was palpable. We rode beside each other for two sets of lights, and his happiness grew with each signal of green, wind on his skin. I caught his eye, but he was his own world. I still liked his brief appearance in mine.

It made me think of my cat, here, on the mat. Clearly overweight, my love had told me to withhold. But I did not need all the tuna, and despite our vet's best advice and her mild allergy to fish, I set the tin before her, heard the scape of metal on slate. Afterward, she stretched and curled in the sun, a full circle of happiness, a black and white swirl of contentment next to the couch.

This morning, when I sat in the sun, there had been so much silence. Part of me felt greedy, lurched toward it. But then I let the bees find their way through the flowers in front of me. I let the everlastings nod their pretty, fading heads. I let the crow come and go in the birdbath. I let the grass dry and summer come and clouds disperse.

I think if I had a long tongue, I'd have set it to the wind.

Fig Tree in Passing

flesh of fruit
twisted logic of limbs
long in light

the bright bark of me
winter of roots
wide sigh of silence

soft stratosphere
orb and curve
slow water-thought

mouth my music
hold, hear
the old in my song.

Derbarl Yerrigan Addresses Mooro Katta

(or, The Swan River Addresses Mount Eliza)

I am   metallic in winter
mercurial answer to sky

in me the black swan
lends fragility of feather
pushing webbed feet down
into my warm body steeped deep
with tannin and leaf

salt-veined and restless
shadow to your light
the black in the blue   day's
diffuse season

curbed by cars   wild
rush toward sea
I am at the foot of your
face   the cliff of it
reading you
leaf by living leaf.

Kings Park

I think someone is seeding hope

one species at a time   and as I slow-move in the sun through stratas
of life there is a shift   that lets me breathe the air of our future
though the city swells around me   all things stay possible

Wattle birds fend off a crow until its black body slow-dives through low
sky   bees peek up skirts of flowers   sky withholds light
from the river but reminds it of rain

she said *I don't know what a prayer is*   but I think she did
lying down in that gift of grass   and here I am learning prayers too

one seed at a time.

Park in Spring

   the Shelducks have returned
           to perch   web-footed
                                      disjoined
  in the high branches of a Tuart

beneath the mighty tree
purple and yellow
laughed out loud.

Redtails

in the morning   in the sun
the redtails
calling across canopy
see-saw songs   a ping-pong game
two notes played – sky's
unoiled door

in morning sun
after days of rain
the world remembers
itself   expands
while the redtails
drunk with sun
curl into each other
dark commas
in stanzas of blue

ping-pong notes
see-saw songs
lift my eyes
to the unoiled morning
sun-lazy the small flock
let me close
bodies turn in light
set leaf and limb
on fire.

V. Perspective

Grass Tree in Sunlight after Rain

explosion of cosmos
each clear star   suspended
white-fire in winter cold

slow-growing firework
strata of sunlight
low galaxy of green

in this paused orbit
now's precise light
see it becoming

So That I May Ask the Morning

I come to you, turning
my pale structure
to your sun

I come to you
not asking, not waiting
just holding the whole of you there
like the memory of water
the promise
of rain

reach me in dreams
draw me up, think me strong
in dreams I will be bold, live bigger
so that I may ask the morning – *please* –
that I may open to the morning
see its goodness, unfurl

and in its gold-ness
become new.

The Sky Runs Right Through Us

North Fremantle

we've got reasons to laugh out loud
salt hangs in the towels on the line

the air between us has shifted
the house is filled with our lightness and warmth
we've got reasons to laugh
(out loud)

the smell of your skin wakes my senses
the smell of your skin stirs my memory
the smell of your skin wakes my senses
your silhouette strong in the hallway

the skin on your arm is touching
the sky is incredibly far away but
the blueness runs right through us, see
the water run right round us
sand stays in bathers on the line

we grow in the light of the morning
the air between us has shifted
summer scents tug at a memory
when the light on my skin was dancing
and I could taste the taste of salt on your skin

we've got reasons to laugh out loud
our house is filled with lightness and peace
the smell of your skin wakes my senses
as we grow in the light of the morning.

Love Letter

This morning quiet birds were filling our trees, in limbs of gum you planted for your Dad, pendulous blossoms still filled with nectar. As you made our coffees in the kitchen, sun found its way once again over blue range in the distance, world of foliage turning gold, deep and bright.

    After you brought me my coffee, I watched the feasting continue, cat crouched amongst the flowers, puffed and whiskered against the cold. Clouds were stretching thin nets until their underbellies were pink and glowing, and the grey that seemed to own them gave way...

    It was then I wanted to stop you, sit you down, show you, but you were off on your bike, gate shuddering where you closed it, kiss lingering in the tissue of my lips.

    And most days I manage to hold it, finding my own traces of grey, humming that song you played me, remember when you told me one of us will die inside these arms. And I own that beautiful tension,

      feeling in that weave

                how fine, so fine, our thread.

Cabbage Moth

all winter I planted memories of spring
amongst the worms, so when the sun

finally pulls away from its lust for North
and returns to me, I realize I had

forgotten what could fly between green
stalks; twenty, thirty soft

mouths that eat at the heart
of my idea of beauty, yet

you need not ask my forgiveness
when your white paper wings

fold and unfold like light
whispered, from your spine

your tiny book
opens

What the Rain Said

what the rain said I cannot say, but I feel her self seep into marrow
like water wills a seed
what the rain said I cannot tell you, but all around us
this thunderous applause yelling *life! life!* hammering it all home
in the triumphant garden

what the rain said it did not whisper but drummed into us
all shouts and fists until there was no speaking, there was no later
just enormous pause of our now, paucity of skin electric
to her entry standing hairs on end
and our silence

what the rain said she said again and again
until we could not forget, would not walk away
could not take our eyes off her entrance
left me raw, animal
gracious with gratitude

what the rain said softened
something final in me, opened to her grief
in those long hot days, long dry weeks
together parched and waiting
like a lizard knows
                      and is afraid

Fitzroy Crossing

this land has made space for me
and deep in its embrace
I rise from sleep
reawakened to light
reawakened to space
alive to colour

old, round rocks
hold deep water secrets –
a landscape's silent memory

so down, down I go
into its
hot, red
heart.

He Sat with a Stone and Called it Love

(a reaction to a poet's keynote speech in Sydney)

'I am mind. From cell of skull I imagine myself expansive, ideas spreading out, neurons racing creating a space cavernous and clean. This I will occupy as 'I'. From this mind spine hangs, body an afterthought, pale and paunched, muscles resigned to minor movements. This face is not for the sun.

    One day I wrote about a stone. The stone sat on my desk and spoke of rivers, rain, tectonic movements before my time. I sat with the stone for days and called it love. This stone was absorbed into the room of myself and I say with this work I have entered into connection, written myself into the world, while still not opening a window.

    One day I wrote about a woman. The woman was under me in a shed, young and supple, red hair flaming in fragments of light. I sat with the memory for days and called it love. The girl was absorbed into the room of myself and I say with this work I have entered into connection, written myself into others, while still not opening a window.'

Perspective Passes over Us

Northcliffe

you can't see
the satellites in the city
it shines too bright
but the swift, secret orbit
carries on

over our roof
the Saucepan, Southern Cross
Orion, those Seven Sisters
come and go
unremarked

but here

we are silenced.

Smog, Delhi (2016)

the earth's dirty laundry
aired, clouds
once-white sheets spread
now grimed by habit, haze
horizon to horizon

from plane's height
there is no hiding
just the facts laid bare
ghosting buildings
fudging fields

from window seat
scape of sky-pillows
lethal, people-stained
the bed we've made

In Delhi They Let Sleeping Dogs Lie

North on Uttar Pradesh Road, a five year-old hoists her infant brother as he slides down childish hip, steps into six lanes of traffic, holds her free hand out to a car's closed window. Spotting a tourist bus, she turns, flashes a quick, wry smile, waves for a wide-eyed audience sealed behind glass. As the traffic surges forward, the girl drops a ten rupee note, stops, bends with baby into incoming cars, bus moves forward and she leaves the frame.

At 7 am smog turns the sun into a rising orange where powerlines march steel-faced into their own erasure. Men lean against shutters of shops, chat, stretch backs, sweep streets into piles of warm endings on which the slim forms of hungry dogs lie. On the corner, old woman threads marigolds with quick flesh of fingers, long needle and line of string, stall keeper lays an arc of carrots until they form a sun. Kites circle the bending in buildings, look to grey in grandeur, measure the slow circumference of time beyond prime. Down a road, down a half-lit laneway, off an impossibly narrow alley, glow of a tungsten lamp; counter of sweets and six red chairs. A teenage boy cleans a porcelain sink, mirror painting him soft, men dropping discs of puri into gold lake of oil. In silence a holy tree splits two-hundred-year-old timber in a second-storey awning of colonial design.

Main street, an instillation of middle-aged men in sun, lazing on pillows of spice, scent of clove thickening the air. Kite over mosque and flags in breeze, rooftops red with dried roses, blue bicycle rider finds pause, three rings of a temple bell.

Tuesday Waits in Lodtunduh

I don't know where you are, but I feel you coming out dark and rich
feel my thick veins quicken in the shadows.

I don't know where you are, but the velvet crush of night sings to me
and your mouth floats and whispers in it all.
Push my arms out, push my arms out into thin air
to the place where dragonflies mate, a fish's deep water dream.
Push it all out into thin air, a parcel of flesh inviting an answer.

High tides and low songs, skewers of seafood and long, bright boats
your lover's sigh like the breath of babies.
The clouds will court and merge and spill their love down on all
greenery
and sundry, and I will cry out with the push and pull of it all
this tightly wrapped gift unfurling, filling me with the noise of nerves
willing their old biology on.

You can come to me with a flower in your hand as white and yellow
as an egg while its ancient parent pushes up the sky.
Behind my ear this sliced yoke and the whole of you between my legs
motorbike pushing us through lush-ness and chaos.

Who knows where we are when we are climbing
climbing thin bead strings of rain to the light and air and pulse.
Who knows who we are when we hook eyes and you join me in my
skin
when I have split wide into the honest-to-god truth of you
the full circle of your spent self and we are open.

Eyes shut sleeping, I don't know where you are
but I feel you coming out dark and rich and right
feel my thick veins exultant, moving up and through and with
into the day's pale light.

Song to Self

own me, like the space inside a cup
fill me, like sap rises in the sure wood of a lemon tree;
whisper where you come from
I open my ribcage to you like a poor man's door
heal the spaces called 'between'
drown me like a monsoon and I will sink my roots deep
let my branches reach up to love the sun
and know the day

tell me, like the moon tells the tides
pull me, like the season draws thick fruit
claim me, like the hearts of children
be me, and I will
be still.

Poems from this collection are dedicated to the following people:

'The Colour of Friday' – for Brad

'Soar' and 'The Waiting Game' – for Greta

'Weaving Ketupat on Pulu Cheplok' – for Nek Sofia

'Tiger on the Beach' – for Pete Wicks

'Return' – for Nicole Hodgson

'Gecko' – for Nandi Chinna

'Last Tree East on Hartley St' – for Julie Watts and Alejandra Czeschka

'Love Letter' – for Ash

Notes

In 'Parting Glass', the phrase 'beautiful hunger' and the image of the sky shivering were taken from a short poem about Afghanistan written by an asylum seeker student in detention on Christmas Island.

'Termangu-Mangu' was inspired by Neil Young's song 'Falling Off the Face of the Earth' (Prairie Wind).

In 'Echo', the Cocos (Keeling) Island quote sourced from http://darwin-online.org.uk/content/frameset?viewtype=text&itemID=A588&pageseq=1

Reference for the newspaper quote at the beginning of 'First Flight': Asylum-seekers reach remote Cocos Islands. (2012, May 16). *The Australian*. Retrieved from http://www.theaustralian.com.au/national-affairs/immigration/asylum-seekers-reach-remote-cocos-islands/story-fn9hm1gu-1226357963033

Reference for the Charles Darwin quote at the beginning of 'Soar': Kerrigan, M. (2005)'. *Charles Darwin's The Voyage of the Beagle: The Journals that Revealed Nature's Grand Plan*. Glasgow, Saraband (Scotland) Limited (p. 190).

In 'Tiger on the Beach', 'Na 'aumakua' refers to 'ancestor spirit'. Hawaiians from the Ka'u district believe believe that some sharks are the embodied form of ancestors. For more information see: http://dlnr.hawaii.gov/sharks/files/2014/07/APaperbyHerbKane.pdf

Reference for the quote by Rumi in 'The Will of Water': Barks, C. (Translator) (2004). *The Essential Rumi*. New York: Harper Collins. (p. 36).

Reference for the quote by John Howard in 'The Will of Water': Immigration Museum. (2001). John Howard's 2001 election campaign policy launch speech. Retrieved from http://museumvictoria.com.au/immigrationmuseum/discoverycentre/identity/videos/politics-videos/john-howards-2001-election-campaign-policy-launch-speech/

Quote from Rolf Jacobson in 'Song for Silence' is from the poem 'The Silence Afterwards' (trans. Roger Greenwald), *North in the World: Selected Poems of Rolf Jacobsen*, University of Chicago Press.

Acknowledgements

I would like to thank first and foremost the women, men and children who shared their lives with me while seeking asylum on Christmas and the Cocos (Keeling) Islands. You helped me to become a better person.
A previous version of this manuscript, entitled *Returning to Land*, was shortlisted for the 2015 Dorothy Hewett Award for an Unpublished Manuscript. Sections of this collection also formed part of a creative writing honours thesis written on the Islands through Curtin University.

Of the poems, 'My Father Comes to the Island' was shortlisted for the 2017 Grieve Poetry Prize, 'What the Rain Said' was commended in 2016 Ethel Webb Bundell Literary Awards, 'Love Letter' won second prize in the 2016 Poetry d'Amour Love Poetry Contest, 'Autumn at the Cidery' was highly commended in the 2015 Love Poetry Contest, 'Black Stone' was commended in the 2015 Katherine Susannah Pritchard Poetry Prize, 'Parting Glass' was shortlisted for the 2014 ACU Poetry Prize, 'Measuring Loss' was highly commended in the 2012 Ethel Webb Bundell Literary Awards, 'Song to Self' was commended in the 2010 Trudy Graham Literary Award for Poetry and 'New Eyes at Wet Night Intersection' won the 2010 Ethel Webb Bundell Literary Award.

Poems in this collection first appeared in the following publications: *Westerly, Westerly New Creative, Cordite, borderlands e-journal, Rhyming the Dead, Cuttlefish, dotdotdash, Regime, Poetry d'Amour, Poetica, Prayers of a Secular World, Grieve Anthology, Recoil Six, The Language of Compassion, Suburban Archaeology, Going Down Swinging, Green Magazine, Famous Reporter* and *WA Botanic Garden: Celebrating 50 Years*.

My sincere gratitude goes to Terri-ann White for her openness and depth of insight into this body of work. Thanks also to Suvendrini Perera, Julienne Van Loon, Roland Leech, Shane McCauley, Pia Smith, Amanda Joy, Georgia Richter and Wendy Jenkins for their input into parts, or all, of this manuscript. A big thank you to Mike Ladd and the staff at Radio National for believing in this collection so early on. My sincere gratitude to the OOTA writers and Hubble Street crew (Julie Watts, Dick Alderson, Carolyn Abbs and Jan Napier) for their care, support and eye for fine detail, to my web-angel Nicole Hodgson, as well as the beautiful men and violinist that are the Ragged Suns, for breathing music into my words.

My love and heartfelt gratitude go to Liana Joy Christenson, Annamaria Weldon and Horst Kornberger for their creative nurturing. I would particularly like to thank my wise women Jennifer Kornberger and Nicole Setton, as well as my grandparents Colin and Mary Hooper. I hold the examples of these fine people close. Thank you Mum, Brad, Janelle, Gail and Brice for believing in me, and lastly, to Ash and Gret who make everything worth it.

www.ingramcontent.com/pod-product-compliance
Lightning Source LLC
Chambersburg PA
CBHW020335170426
43200CB00006B/388